The Last Stone in the Circle

D1603447

Irena Praitis

Grateful acknowledgment is made to the editors of the journals in which the following poems have appeared or are forthcoming:

American Athenaeum: "Stripped"
Raintown Review: "The Finer Things," "Fall In," "Fear Itself," "I Asked For It," "Life's Fine," "Some Men Rise," "For Love of the Game," appear in slightly different versions as the sonnet crown "Jack Fell Down"
Slipstream: "Coda" published as "The Sand Cave"
Nothing to Declare: A Guide to the Flash Sequence, from White Pine Press: "Bread, I. II. III. IV. V." appear in a slightly different format
Southwest Review: "Chord," published as "Lyrics"
Common Ground Review: "Body Box Detail," "Walked On"
Hawai'i Pacific Review: "Animals," "Columbarium," "Déaþ"
Saranac Review: "Thin Skinned," "The Low Sky"
Two Hawks Quarterly: "Cap," "Sere," "Vision"

ISBN 978-0-9908047-6-5

Printed in the United States of America

RED MOUNTAIN PRESS

Santa Fe, New Mexico

www.redmountainpress.us

ACKNOWLEDGMENTS

Special thanks to the United States Holocaust Memorial
Museum and especially Huddy B. Haller, who first
answered my request for information, and William
Connelly who provided assistance and open access to
research materials used in this book.

A heartfelt thanks to Junis Sultan who provided many
translations of Gert Stoi's research, several of which are
used in this book.

Thank you to Elle Mooney for a careful and heartfelt
consideration of this collection.

Thanks to Wyn Cooper for tightening the manuscript and
sharpening the poems.

Many thanks to Arthur Vogelsang whose feedback inspired
new areas of exploration.

Warm thanks to April Ossmann whose careful reading and
generous commentary strengthened the poems.

Thank you, Alberto Ríos, for all the insights you've shared
over the years.

Gratitude to California State University, Fullerton, for
support during the writing of this book. Special thanks to
my colleagues and especially my students who serve as a
continual source of inspiration.

Thank you, Denise Low, for choosing this book for the Red Mountain Poetry Prize.

Warm thanks to Susan Gardner who gives her whole heart to Red Mountain Press and the wonderful books it publishes. You make the poetry landscape more beautiful.

Mom, Dad, Judy, Vida, Janine, Dave, Roger, Aidan, Garrett, Colin, Eric, Karl, Kendall, and Ezra—you are the best family.

Ishaan, Ishaan, Ishaan thank you for all the light you bring.

For Aleksandras Misevičius

*Born in Vilkija, Lithuania, October 17, 1908, who died April
7, 1944 in Römhild, one of Buchenwald's 174 sub-camps*

*And for my brother
Edward Praitis
Born: Omaha, NE, July 12, 1964
Died: Seattle, WA, November 12, 2013*

TABLE OF CONTENTS

ACKNOWLEDGMENTS   3

PROLOGUE   11

I   13

CHORD   15

I CAN'T BREATHE   17

THE FINER THINGS: PORTRAIT OF A *KAPO*   18

COLUMBARIUM   19

CLOWNS   21

TAKE *S*   23

THIN-SKINNED   27

BREAD   28

MISSING ITS RING   29

COBBLING LESSONS   31

ONE, THEN   34

FOR THE DEAD   35

I ASKED FOR IT: PORTRAIT OF A *KAPO*   38

ARION ATER   39

STRIPPED   41

RUE   42

WE WORE CAIN   43

II   45

DA CAPO AL CODA   47

SUPPORT   48

BREAD   49

LIFE'S FINE: PORTRAIT OF A *KAPO*   50

BODY BOX DETAIL   51

WALKED ON   52

BREAKING STONE   53

FALL IN: PORTRAIT OF A *KAPO*   57

CLOTHES   58

ANIMALS   59

FEAR ITSELF: PORTRAIT OF A *KAPO*   61

BREAD   62

EXCAVATION   63

III   69

VISION   71

CAP   72

SERE   73

FOR LOVE OF THE GAME: PORTRAIT OF A *KAPO*   74

DÉAÞ   75

BREAD   77

OUTSIDE THE CIRCLE   78

SOME MEN RISE: PORTRAIT OF A *KAPO*   79

THE LOW SKY   80

FOREST CEMETERIES   81

BREAD   84

CODA   85

NOTES   89

Most of us perceive Evil as an entity, a quality that is inherent in some people and not in others. Bad seeds ultimately produce bad fruits as their destinies unfold.... Upholding a Good-Evil dichotomy also takes "good people" off the responsibility hook. They are freed from even considering their possible role in creating, sustaining, perpetuating, or conceding to the conditions that contribute to delinquency, crime, vandalism, teasing, bullying, rape, torture, terror, and violence.

—*Philip G. Zimbardo*

With numbing regularity good people were seen to knuckle under the demands of authority and perform actions that were callous and severe. Men who are in everyday life responsible and decent were seduced by the trappings of authority, by the control of their perceptions, and by the uncritical acceptance of the experimenter's definition of the situation, into performing harsh acts. A substantial proportion of people do what they are told to do, irrespective of the content of the act and without limitations of conscience, so long as they perceive that the command comes from a legitimate authority.

—*Stanley Milgram*

PROLOGUE

Thank you for your patience. According to the documentation we have found, Alexander Misewitsch, born in Wilkia on October 17, 1908, died at Römhild on April 7, 1944. His cause of death was listed as tuberculosis. He is buried in the Waldfriedhof in Römhild.

We have now completed our research on this request.

September 5, 2011

I

We were received by the camp commandant…

who told us with the help of an interpreter:

"The camp Römhild

is not like Buchenwald.

It goes faster here…"

CHORD

Listen:
music travels far
on quiet nights.

Open the windows,
enjoy another man's opera,
your neighbor's wife
singing at her bath.

Listen,
death can't not be
musical,

pick axes clanging,
kapos beating,
one last breath
guttering the throat
of the no longer living.

Listen

for my entrance.

I've timed it

beautifully.

I CAN'T BREATHE

We string words.

Winter robins
hunting seeds.

One word?
Answers.

Two words?
A plea.

Three pearls
in a chokehold

rest in peace.

THE FINER THINGS: PORTRAIT OF A *KAPO*

You expect fine things: rich food,
rare wine, soft clothes, long baths?
Me, too. Here luxury means sleeping
off the floor, a few more grams
of bread, a sturdy pair of shoes.
You grow accustomed to the thud
a truncheon makes, the shock a kick
sends up your leg. Not that I like it.
No, no, I'm not some sadist.
I made a choice between beating
or being beaten. Who wouldn't?
No back breaking work, more soup,
warmer feet come winter, surviving
to see spring. Don't think I am not you.

COLUMBARIUM

Unboxed
from the casket
of civilian clothes
everything burns:

disinfection,
the prison tunic,
beatings,
the cold,

the fear
that drives me
to obey
commands
meant for dogs,

the shame
of lying, thieving,
putting others
in harm's way.

In my survival
cell I
speak little,
help no one.

The ash
of my flesh
settles denser,
stickier than
the powder
of crucibled
trees flying
on the wind's breath,
speckled with bone
fragments
too splintered
to shore up
what I once was.

CLOWNS

If Papa finds out,
he'll kill them.
Then he'll be shot, too,
like Mama and Oscar.
There's just the two of us now.
So I say nothing
about the guards
who paint my face
with soot, black smile
stretching my mouth,
black nose, black eyebrows
crowing above my own.

Dance little clown,
dance, they taunt.
I hunch, spring, hobble
like the men we watched
on holidays who hit each other
all about the head
while we laughed
until we cried.

I hope
some guardsman's duty
will call them,
but it never does.
They stick bottles, broomsticks,
and themselves in me,
laughing, cursing, spitting,
then feed me spoons
of marmalade.

Papa would be proud
that I don't cry
or show my fear.
After, I wipe
the black off
with my sleeves
and practice songs
Mama and Oscar
taught me.

I sing for Papa,
too tired to be angry
at my clowning.
One day I'll be so good
I'll make him smile.

TAKE *S*

I swing the sledge while working the mine.

As we

descend

the rough-

sawn stairs

our work

clogs thresh

the fine

wood grain—

starving men

who cannot eat

grain stairs offer.

We reach

the pit

to scatter

amidst

the blasted

basalt.

I wonder

while I work:

What would

the SS be

     without

one S?

     I shift

my grip:

     and struck

becomes

     the truck

that drives

     me homeward.

     A rock slam

on a guard

     can send me

on the lam—

     or end me.

     Hands

melt snow

     to spark

the greening
of spring now.

No wind
in sails
ails me.
I don't fret:
Pearls before swine
might still
yield wine.

One stone turned
becomes the tone
that sets me
singing:

Sweep
away slights,
and sleep
with sin,
hold love
skin-deep.

Sadist,

redeemer,

      which would

it be,

      if laughter

rests

      one letter

away from

      slaughter?

THIN-SKINNED

Teasing
drove her to tears.
A neighbor's cold shoulder
fluttered her for weeks.
War scraped her thin.

I read to her
while her needle clicked
buttons, pressed damp
cloths to her forehead
during bombing raids.

I drove
without permission
after my neighbor called
to say my sister
spent all morning

patting a bucket,
clucking to chickens
who were no longer there.

BREAD

I. *First Morning in Camp*

I see, across the gray hunched backs of prisoners frantic
over food, my brother walking his way, shoulders
squared against a backdrop of summer leaves. He kicks
a man, cursing at him to eat faster. The man scrabbles in
the gravel after spilled soup. My brother turns—not my
brother, a stranger in prison stripes, his build so like
Mikhail's my throat aches. He catches me staring. I bend
over my bread watching his shoes—not clogs, not rags:
shoes.
What're you looking at? He slams the truncheon then
grabs my bread. He's Russian, like me. I lash out. *What
is with you? You're not an animal. You're one of us!* He
drives his knee into my chin. My teeth clamp on nothing.
He seethes: *I'm not one of you. I'm alive. This stick means
I'll stay that way. You? You're a dead man. You couldn't
even keep your head down or hold your first day's bread.* I hiss
back, *When I see my wife I'll meet her eyes without the shame
of what I've done haunting me.* He laughs. *You're new.
You'll learn—if you live long enough.* My would-be brother
spits as he walks away.

MISSING ITS RING

I lie still
after the beating.
Piaf,
"Mon Légionnaire,"
limps about
my mind.

My hand,
missing its ring,
trembles
along the table.

With this fist
I beat my wife,
dinner late,
coffee cold.

Nights she'd press
her broken lip
to my cheek,
beloved—
as I thrust,

a new pair of heels...
and I promised her
anything
as she clutched me
with desire,
or forgiveness,

or love—

I have always been angry.

Green summer days
girls' dresses
parasoled around them.

I threw stones,
hating
such sweetness.

COBBLING LESSONS

Naked, you
hold your shoes
and clothes
against your chest,
waiting for the head shave
and shower.

Across the yard
you watch
a prisoner work
the dried
blood stiffness
from a rag
he winds around
his foot, deft
as a violinist
bowing.
Cloth rust
resins his palms.
You think of your father
cobbling shoes.

Kneeling, intent,
cradling your foot,
running his thumb
along the heel's smile,

tracing the arch
with a forefinger,
he'd read bone spurs,
learn gait,
then craft sole,
upper, heel:
awl piercing leather,
waxed thread mated
to curved needle,

stitch matching stitch.

Give me your shoes!

The truncheon
strikes
your shoulders.

Crouching into
the burning

you try not to howl, try

not to breathe, try

not to sear

the vision

in your mind

of his fingers

slipped under

the tongues

of your shoes

as he lifts them

and walks away.

ONE, THEN

Nothing is
as it seems?
No. At the mine's edge
all is as it is.

Death is death
and nothing else:

no stitches to pluck,
no solving for x,

no solution
for the known:
here, then not.

Meaning requires
tiers of significance.

One, then zero.
One, then zero.
All there is.

FOR THE DEAD

I.

Tonight's rain grimes you.

Like after brothels,
the more you wash
the dirtier you feel.
Thinking justifies
but cannot quiet,
cannot cleanse.

Chain smoking through
reasons, you, too, push
the silent to the corners.
No one wants to sleep
with a dead man.

II.

The boxcar opens
on midnight.
Everyone rushes

for rain-soaked air.
An elbow stutters
your windpipe.
You slip in the wet.
A confusion of lights
and commands:
Place the corpses
on the bikes. Quickly! Quickly!
Back to handlebars, seat to seat,
undertaker to a makeshift hearse,
you slog through woods
to a hilltop clearing.

III.

Stumble forward at your name.
Grip the bread, slimed with rain,
a guard shoves toward you.

They shout at the dead man
until you drag him up
for inspection. You jam the bread
a guard insists on giving him
between stiff fingers.

You gnaw your stale dust,
let the rain gather on your lips,
licking the salty wet to ease
dry swallows.

IV.

You pray for morning all night,
crouching in the sand cave,
pant legs muddied
by the puddles,
refusing to sleep
with your corpse.

At dawn, you're greeted
by the dead man
spattered with dirt
kicked up by rain,
hand clutching bread
you don't think of taking,
no matter how hungry you are.

I ASKED FOR IT: PORTRAIT OF A *KAPO*

I barely survived my first beating
at Buchenwald, the worst served up
after I joked about more soup.
Two *kapos* laid into me. My arms
flailed—my eyes, my neck,
my ribs—I failed to protect them.
As the coals of their teaching
rained down on me, I faced
the last stone in the circle.
Consciousness hobbled back.
I learned my lesson. My body
crucibled, I swore: *never again.*
Transferred here, no one offered me
this truncheon. I asked for it.

ARION ATER

In out of the way hamlets,
Wolfmannshausen, Westenfeld,
Haina, dark wood and white
plaster houses queue up
as they have for centuries
along swept sidewalks
and winding cobbled streets.
Red and pink geraniums
thrive in window boxes.

Beside the restless wheat
and neatly spaced
vineyards quilting hills,
not a single stray leaf
skitters along the Autobahn.

But in the forests, haunted
by solitary birches and tales
of the brothers Grimm,
mobs of beech, firs, linden, and oak,
lord over riotous bracken,
ferns rife at the knee.

Above, sunlight
batters the cage
of vegetation
but can't break through.

Leaving slime trails
across endless rot
from countless seasons
re-dampened
by afternoon rain,

large slugs, black and shiny
as crude, glisten
on tissue flaked
from forest sentries,
feasting on decay.

STRIPPED

Nobody speaks of the dead man
who troubles our sleep, his feet free
of their rags, half fetal, elbows to knees,
one hand cupping the other,
like a child, almost at peace.
In the semi-darkness, we tear
strips from his shirt to wrap our feet.
I sleep beside him three nights
as he molts, bare from our foraging.
I tolerated the innocence
of his nakedness, until the stink drove
me to report. Now my body ends the row,
one comrade watches my back
as I sleep in a dead man's bed.

Rue

Climbing toward

the camp,

do you see

rue tangled

in proliferation

along your route,

trampled underfoot?

Or, in this place,

can you gain

nothing

from symbolic

gestures?

WE WORE CAIN

> *Whoever slayeth Cain, vengeance shall be taken on him sevenfold.*
>
> —*King James Bible*

Red cords wreathe
kapos' arms.
AEL rides
each man's back.
Who doesn't bear
the mark of Cain here?
Slamming shovels
against resistant stone,
beating, being beaten:
No one keeps
a brother.
Abel long dead,
each Cain
kills another
and all of us suffer
vengeance sevenfold.

II

"Here, you bear the beating or you die."

Da Capo al Coda

The path funnels you
into the sand cave's mouth.

Two columns of limping
prisoners ordered inside:

35 sets of twins shuffling
through at a slant.

The mountain's brow
domes above you;

your coda:
not so large

as history,
just the size

of one man leading
one man

out of this world.

SUPPORT

Every day the worst luck! Ordered to drag the dying to
the pit. Call me the new-age Charon of this underworld.
By tonight, tomorrow at the outside, this lug will reach
forgetfulness. Not me. I remember everyone I've hauled,
Frenchman, Serb, Russian, Pole—all the sorry bastards
sap my strength as they go under. No one ever thanks
me. I don't receive extra rations. If the mine, or the
beatings, or the shits don't kill me, surely dragging along
the dead will.

BREAD

II. *Lost on the March*

Near the road, a farmer swings his arm. Another stone
thrower? I duck. The boy beside me catches a potato. I
grab his wrist, bite his fingers. He screams and beats my
temple with his free hand, but I don't let go, salivating
from the rusty salt of his blood. He loosens his grip and I
shove the potato in my mouth. He cradles his hand
jostled by other prisoners. He's young, maybe eleven,
skeletal, like all of us, Russian, like me. I don't look at
him long. He lags and I lose him, his blood snaking
down my chin. Over the bent backs of stumbling
prisoners my would-be brother smirks at me—toppled
from *kapo*, bereft of his truncheon, forced to march
without food, he's not quick enough to steal this mealy
tuber caked in dirt. I swallow, trying not to gag. I don't
know if the sobbing I hear comes from the boy I bit or
some other lost soul about to lose his sorry life for
lagging. A rifle's report cuts the mourning.

LIFE'S FINE: PORTRAIT OF A *KAPO*

I didn't ask to be a *kapo*,

but I didn't say no.

What's the difference?

In the camp, humanity's distilled.

The good grow brutish,

the brutish survive. People

who sing, who share bread,

who shout and encourage?

The cunning take advantage.

The best die. Some bear beatings

stone-faced. Others shriek for mercy.

No one cares. Friends? Liabilities.

Partners, enemies, what can be of use.

In every case, life exacts its fine.

BODY BOX DETAIL

I bring the crate to haul the bastards out.
Not a bad job. You learn not to think.
Get it done. Do it well. There's the stench,
but what doesn't stink around here?
Latrines, barracks—some prisoners smell
worse than the dead. This morning, a problem:
three bodies, one box. I toss in the first,
lay the second feet to head, and shove it down,
stubborn, won't bend much—then head to feet
with the third. Damned lid won't close.
I shake, push, shove, slam the case.
No good. I step up. Walk head to foot,
foot to head—pops, cracks, strange thuds—
the lid snaps into place.

WALKED ON

I've never known a life without you.
We ran the gray rib of our backstreet,
gossiping mothers stretching
laundry across alleyways.
Hot summer days in the river,
boasting about sex,
stealing paper from the office,
we resisted together, were caught,
sang *Chant du Départ*,
faced punishment,
arrived here.

He hops on the coffin
and stomps you in.
That's what makes you gone,
not death—but being walked on.

BREAKING STONE

*Breathe! Breathe
hard!* She pleads.

I say nothing.
Nothing.

My tongue frozen
to the lamppost,
children laughing.

Mother scolded,
tossed the bloody
towel in the sink
after wiping
my chin.

Move bastard!
But I can't
unclench,
fingers sutured
to the metal
by the cold.

The *kapo*
slams my ear
and the hands
obey, robbed
of a few layers
of skin.

I say nothing,
pick up
the shovel—
hands burning,
along coarse wood—
smash with the blade,
kick the rocks

to a ragged pile,
swallow silt,
re-level my edge
against the next stone.

Preempting
Sisyphus—
No test against
a mountain.
No height gained.

Every boulder
gestating heroics
crushed.
No comfort
in a predictable
misery, always
the unexpected.

I don't deserve this!
Why me?
I hear the others.

I say nothing.
Who doesn't have
a crime to expiate?

I will break
until I break
the tears
I did not shed

for my boy,

dead at birth,
my tongue

swollen,
saying
nothing
(nothing!)

while his mother
rocking,

keened,
hands clenching
bloody sheets,
the cord
tight as a noose
around his neck.

FALL IN: PORTRAIT OF A *KAPO*

What rules if we each fall into our own line?
I obey. What choice is there? I refused
to swing the truncheon, but *kapos* spit
and swore at me, beating me until
I followed commands. I didn't hit
hard. I didn't hit hard until now,
until this man, this worm, this sniveling pig
who pissed without permission.
He drops his pants. He pleads.
I hate the way he squirms. I slam
my stick until his scalp splits—
two *kapos* call me off. I smash
my way through the stupid cows staring
over their shovels. I could beat them all.

CLOTHES

In the pall before sleep, I'm haunted
by the clothes I wore, stored in the garret
like my heir-apparent ghost. Who will fill
the sleeves scratched threadbare by my unbruised
elbows? Will the tweeds be passed out to the poor,
or to day laborers, grateful for the warmth,
my trousers lasting longer at the knees
of another man? Perhaps they'll be delivered,
a non-descript brown package surprising
my sweeping wife about to learn
her widowhood. She'd tug at the packing cord
then choke to find the wedding ring,
the deloused shirt and pants, but not the shoes—
those long since worn by another man.

ANIMALS

The boy pleads
and I remember
mother whipping me
with the vacuum cord
after she caught me
making farting noises
with friends.
You're not an animal!
Hide your dirt
or you'll be buried in it—
Small decencies designed
to save us
now cost us our lives.

Come with me to ask. Please!
I need to go outside... he whines.

Use the barrel! I snap.
He starts to cry.
A boy sent to fight,
caught like the rest of us.

I turn on the dirt floor,

but listen for his voice.

The night guard slaps him

with the rifle as he begs.

I hear his bowels loosen

as the guard cocks the gun

and fires, grunting with disgust.

FEAR ITSELF: PORTRAIT OF A *KAPO*

Terrified of the neighbor's dog, I refused
to leave our farm. *The only thing worse than fear,*
father thundered, *is showing it!* I pissed
my pants when he beat me. *The dog's more*
scared than you! The most afraid bites first.
Learn something, idiot! I practiced
with my slingshot, stones chipping the fence post,
until one, well-slung, crushed the bitch's eye.
She stopped barking and died soon after.
With my truncheon, I still aim for the eye
or the groin. No one knows I work
to hold my water, my bowels,
when I raise the stick for that first strike,
but they never see me the same way again.

BREAD

III. *Our Route Turns*

They herd us near a farmhouse. Shouting, thrashing, I
claw shoulders. Wood splinters, liquid sloshes. *Kraut!* I
fight toward food. Cursing guards slam a pathway with
their guns. They grab three men, beating them to their
knees before a broken barrel, pickling leaking from its
sides. In the mud a cabbage, gouged by one bite mark,
unfolds like a rose. A guard shoots each man through the
skull. The third man's jaw is blown off, my would-be
brother, who falls away from me.

EXCAVATION

In 1947, after a Soviet-led investigation, a mass grave
was uncovered in a sand cave mineshaft near the
former work education labor camp outside of Römhild,
Germany. Officials estimate 70 prisoners were killed
or buried alive in the cave.

Winter's the worst
time to dig,
but this work
will not wait

for a kinder season.

> With the increased use of
> foreign labor, and other
> workers in military and
> economically important plants,
> there are increasing cases of
> refusal to work, which must be
> counteracted in the interest
> of the military force of the
> German people by any means.

My wife,
scarred by war,
turns from
my battle stench,

Alle zusammen Kinder!

wrapped in
wintry distance.

I rage my pick
into frozen ground

until I'm steaming
in the cold.

eins, zwei, Polizei!

I knock through first.
My miner's lamp
flashes cave walls.

Workers who refuse to work or
jeopardize the work ethic in
any way must be taken into
police custody to maintain

64

order and security, and are to
be held in specific labor
education camps.

A skull
gapes at me,
jaw dropped
at my arrival.

     drei, vier, Offizier!

Two long bones
descend from a pelvis,
a shipwrecked hull
of ribs

still shrouded
in torn prison clothes,
arches from the ground,
the heart long gone.

     fünf, sechs, alte Hex!

A crutch
propped against the wall
angles above a skull

balanced on

a shoulder.

> The labor camp workday is to
> last no fewer than 10 hours
> and no more than 12 hours. The
> maximum length of sentence is
> to be 56 days.

Enclaves

hold skeletons,

arm bones

still curved

around each other

in some agony

they can

no longer share.

> *sieben, acht, gute Nacht!*

Deep

in the cave

I find

skeletons

laid with care

head to foot,

> The work camps are exclusively
> to accommodate listless
> elements whose behavior is
> equivalent to work sabotage.
> The incarceration is intended
> for an educational purpose, it
> shall not serve as a punitive
> measure.

prepared

by someone

sealed in,

stripped of hope

but not compassion,

lost

to this world.

neun, zehn, auf Wiedersehen!

III

After a half century I still ask myself: Were our dead buried with dignity and have they been honored in the course of the years?

VISION

Above ground
between
the wheel ruts
one dead mole,
dark as the earth
it turns to,
fur soft
as ash,
against the gray
basalt—
others claw
below ground.

CAP

They shave your head, line you up
under their perforated-pipe shower,
peck at you on your crawl toward roll call.
They scratch your number in their ledger,
stack you clogs, striped trousers, a rag-
patched shirt, one round cap. Laundered
in another era, threadbare, who'd wear
these clothes—prisoners? Criminals?
Men like you? We all need warmth to survive.
A cold wind fingers your razor-rashed scalp.

You shoulder your prisoner's shirt,
pull on pants, curl your toes to grooves
in another man's shoes.
                    But you will not
wear a dead man's hat to save your head.

SERE

The mountain will bask,
sun-warmed and green,
in the summer we won't see.

The local innkeeper
once advertised
a fairy grotto
in the sand cave
where we store shovels
to bury our dead.

Beyond the barbed wire,
gold leaves spin
through shafts
of sunlight.
Leaves, not snow.

How we will ache
when it comes,
from the cold,
for the sere
beauty of it.

FOR LOVE OF THE GAME: PORTRAIT OF A *KAPO*

Hear the beauty in morning roll call pain?

Palms sweating, heart racing, I salivate,

grow hard. Twitching, I barely contain myself.

Patience. With breakfast laggards I begin.

Bodies spasm under beatings, freed

from the mind. Slaps on skin, welts

blossoming, my grunts, their begging,

synchronized. Show me your animal.

Call out mine. With each blow I skirt

the precipice where their pain and my pleasure

climax. Blood courses through my limbs.

The rush slams my ears, cock swollen—

hold the ecstasy. Hold the agony.

With that first beating, I knew my calling.

Déaþ

No hood.
No scythe.
No skeletal finger tap.

No ill will.
No sweet escape.
No justice.

No rhyme.
No reason.
No reckoning.

No why—

Nothing human.

Up against oblivion
who wouldn't insist on
a person,
some pernicious soul
to shake a fist at,
try and condemn,

some force
to bend around
our sense of purpose
or fairness?

Nothing's
incomprehensible.

Not enough presence
for indifference.

One blank
we constantly finger
but never inscribe.

BREAD

IV. *After the War*

He licked off the butter then chewed the bread heel, bite
by bite, my son. Marya's scolding never changed him,
strong and stubborn, like me. Villagers ran for the
woods, but Marya they shot against the southern wall,
Ivan holding her hand, too stunned to cry. My neighbor
buried them. *At least you know they're here*, he condoles as
I fold over their grave intending to stay forever. But I
know I won't die here blanketing them. The selfish
animal that kept me alive (for what? for this?) will not
release me now.

OUTSIDE THE CIRCLE

Clothes fray, clogs splinter,
basalt slivers skin.
The same fifty soup bowls
pass from lip to lip as we
eat in shifts while guards
blast the mountain stones loose.
We wash in one trough, bear
the *kapos'* beatings, fear the dogs,
shiver alike at morning roll call.
Nights, we shit and piss in the barrel,
waving away the midges,
without a shred of privacy.
But mark this: When we die,
Belgians, French, and Dutch
rest in the town cemetery,
while we cart Russians and Poles
to makeshift forest graves.
After sharing hell, God forbid
our bones should mingle.

SOME MEN RISE: PORTRAIT OF A *KAPO*

Father outlasted fate's pestle at Verdun
lecturing me: *Some men rise, other men*
fall. If you stumble, don't show
your face to me. When the guards
offered me the stick, I rose to it.
My beatings do not grind men down,
they crumble before my truncheon
touches them. Fools *let* themselves
be kicked and starved. Though I wear
clogs and prison stripes, I walk
like men with polished shoes, slick
silver buttons ascending their coats. We stand
tall in any circumstance, spitting
on the weak who fall around us.

THE LOW SKY

The camp commandant

When the eastern front
collapses, and the wave
of the red army swallows me,
will I survive
like an animal,
or die
like a human being?

Outside my window,
kapo savages beat
hunched prisoners tromping
to the mine. They squabble
over food, splash in the washing
trough. Furtive, cunning when questioned,
cow-like during roll call,
maybe not animals entirely,
(they *look* like people)
but not human, certainly.

More allied planes overhead.
The low sky spits
against the panes.

FOREST CEMETERIES

I. *Lower Forest Cemetery*

Even when I turn the wrong way
I find you, a patch of graves
at the foot of the mountain,
sunk beneath waves of waist-
high weeds and biting nettles
parched by sun.

Propped from without
by stout sticks,
your fence bows outward
and earthward
with expansive force.

Two wooden benches,
slats broken, imply visitors
though no one could sit here
without strained balance.

(Too small, this plot,
too small to hold

so many, but somehow
the earth manages.)

Defiant, unkempt,
without ceremony
without care,

no maintenance for you,
steadfast as death.

I breathe you in.
You're not angry,
but you're not at peace.
Awake. Raw. Jaw set,

never needing to exhale.

II. *Upper Forest Cemetery*

Different, but not
opposite, you're quieter.
Moss greens
the rough rectangles
along the ground

sketched out in gray rock
with no body count per box.

Beech leaves rustle over
a bouquet from last spring
or the spring before,
still wrapped in paper
browned brittle by sun and rain,
keeping company with stones.

Firs block your view,
or become it.

You never left the mountain.

I can almost see you—
tired, propped up,
draped on benches—

I walk among you
with nothing in my hands.

BREAD

V. My Would-Be Brother's Widow

I survived. Those I loved did not. Your widow lived
near enough. I needed to walk. Where else would I go?
While your wife clenches her teeth against the pain of
your story, your child bears witness: fierce, unafraid.
Like you. She scoops butter with her fingers glaring at
me with your eyes my would-be brother. Look through
me, friend. See your daughter reject the bread I brought
as if she knew how we fought over it. She survives,
brother. Brother, brother, look through me.

CODA

*On April 1, 1945, injured and ill prisoners unable to
march were separated from the main Römhild work
education camp evacuation group, herded into a sand
cave, shot at, and then sealed inside the mineshaft by
an explosion.*

Leaning my crutch
against the wall
I sink to the ground.

I, the others, we learn
the darkness.
Only blind in sight
we feel our dead,
lay them out,
cross cracked hands
over hearts.

We hold the dying,
those thrashing
to find anchor.
We quiet

the frenzied digging,
the exhausted weeping.

We linger,
a tangle of thoughts
in the mind
of the mountain.

We no longer crawl
to the back of the cave—
urine, feces,
so many of our bowels
diseased.
We'll die breathing
in our piss and shit.

We discover time
for everything.
The appetites of anger
fade away.

Those we loved
might not know us,
but we know each other,

all the evils we live,
the shreds
of decency
we never surrender.

Vlad begins singing
a scrap of tune
from childhood,
a song for lonely days,
for skipping stones
and carefree games.

I remember the world
I will not see—
and think of my son,
how I made the choice
each day,
to hold
his helpless body
in wonder,
and cleanse him
with love.

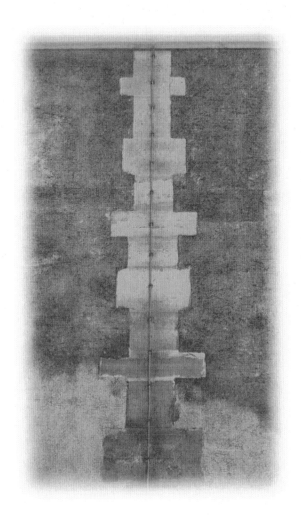

NOTES

Page 11: I first learned of the camp at Römhild from an International Tracing Service response to a query I'd made regarding a relative, my great uncle. The documentation noted that he had died "at Römhild." I'd never heard of Römhild, so I researched and found that this camp was a sub-camp of Buchenwald, one of 174 sub-camps almost all of which I'd never heard of before.

The camp at Römhild opened in September of 1943 and closed with a forced evacuation of prisoners in April of 1945. The camp usually housed around 300 prisoners, mostly French, Polish, and Russian. The camp guards seldom abused anyone. Instead, foremen, or *kapos,* were recruited from the ranks of prisoners. According to the reports of survivors the *kapos* were exceptionally brutal.

Page 13: The poems are informed by first-hand accounts found in Gert Stoi's book, *Das Arbeitserziehungslager Römhild 1943-1945 Dokumentation eines Verbrechens (The Work Education Camp Römhild 1943-1945 Documentation of a Crime).* The section epigraphs are taken from accounts presented in Stoi's book.

Page 15: A Chinese prisoner died at Römhild. The cause of death was listed as phlegmon, but an eyewitness speculated that the man committed suicide reporting, "I saw the Chinese prisoner lying on the floor with his throat cut."

Page 18: A primary infrastructure of the camp was the recruitment of prisoners to serve as *kapos* who abused other prisoners. As one witness noted, "Among the prisoners there were some who were 'handy' and ready to become the hangman of their comrades only to get a second portion of soup."

Page 21: A prisoner recounted, "A five year old Polish boy brought with his father was required to dress up as a clown and dance on command."

Page 27: This poem references an eyewitness who recounted reasons for incarceration, "The committed crimes were that one beat a cow during some agricultural work and another picked cherries from a tree. One who was working on a farm forgot to give a horse a portion of oats. Another man drove, without permission, to his sister who lived 45 kilometers away."

Page 29: The song "Mon Légionnaire," sung by Edith Piaf includes the lyrics, "I don't know his name, I don't know anything about him. / He loved me all night / My legionnaire!" "lost happiness, fleeing happiness," "I dreamt, though, that destiny / would give me back, one bright morning / my legionnaire."

Page 39: *Arion Ater* is the name of a black slug commonly found in the forests of Thuringia. Wolfmannshausen, Westenfeld, and Haina are towns passed when approaching Römhild from the west.

Page 41: This poem is inspired by an eyewitness account, "Without doubt we lived in dirt and in a confusing mess. (I slept three days next to a dead French comrade who had already started to rot.)"

Page 43: AEL, short for Arbeitserziehungslager / work education camp, was sewn onto the prison tunics.

Page 48: This poem emerges from an eyewitness who reported, "Some of the *kapos* disappeared and returned after a short while pulling our ill comrades who could not stand anymore to the rank. Then we began marching again, supporting or carrying our ill comrades between us."

Page 51: This poem emerges from an eyewitness account, "The *kapos* appeared the next morning with a box that was familiar to us and threw our comrade inside."

Page 53: Working conditions were brutal, even without the beatings, "He had to push heavy dump cars with his bare hands in the great cold so that the skin of his hands was snatched off in pieces."

Page 59: An eyewitness recounted the following, "During the evacuation march, a 12 year old Ukrainian boy was shot to death one night when he asked, desperately, to leave the cellar where we were all housed, to relieve himself."

Pages 63-67: The text in Courier New font is a translation of Heinrich Himmler's dictates on Arbeitserziehungslagers. The text in italics presents a traditional German children's rhyme "Eins, Zwei, Polizei" that can be translated as follows,

One, two, police
Three, four, officer
five, six, old witch
seven, eight, good night!
nine, ten, good-bye!

Page 78: The burial practices associated with the camp were strangely political. A witness noted, "The Western people (French, Belgians, Dutch) were buried together in a grave in the cemetery in Römhild. The people from the East were buried in the forest near the camp."

The Last Stone in the Circle is set in Palatino,
a twentieth century font designed by Hermann Zapf
based on the humanist typefaces of the Italian
Renaissance and named for the sixteenth century
Italian master of calligraphy Giambattista Palatino.